In memory of
David B. Biebel
Founder of Healthy Life Press
1949–2018

FOREST OF DREAMS
*SCRIPTURE AND ART TO STRENGTHEN YOUR HEART*
Copyright © 2018 by Dianne Iivari

Published by:

Healthy Life Press, LLC • Bristol, VA 24202
*www.healthylifepress.com*

Author & Artist: Dianne Iivari
Book Design: Judy Johnson
Author Photo: Peridot Photography

Printed in the United States of America

No part of this publication may be reproduced, stored in a retrieval system, or transmitted in any form or by any means—for example, electronic, photocopy, recording—without the prior written permission of the author.

Library of Congress Cataloging-in-Publication Data
**Iivari, Dianne**
**Forest of Dreams: Scripture and Art to Strengthen Your Heart**

ISBN **978-1-939267-70-2**
1. RELIGION / Christian Life / Inspirational
2. RELIGION / Christian Life / Devotional

Bible quotations are from the Holy Bible, New Living Translation, copyright © 1996, 2004, 2007, 2013, 2015 by Tyndale House Foundation. Used by permission of Tyndale House Publishers Inc., Carol Stream, Illinois 60188. All rights reserved.

Most Healthy Life Press resources are available wherever books are sold. Distribution is primarily through *Amazon.com* and *healthylifepress.com*. Multiple copy discounts are available directly from Healthy Life Press. Wholesale distribution of this book is exclusively through *IngramSpark.com* and its affiliate, *SpringArbor.com*. Contact the publisher if you have questions about how to obtain a retailer's discount.

# Dedication

I would like to dedicate this book to God our Father and Creator, who created me and gave me the talent to paint.

I would also like to dedicate this book to my best friend and ex-husband Keith, who always believed in me and my artwork. He is now gone to be with the Lord, with the new heart he so desperately wanted.

Another dedication is to my mom, who believes in me one hundred percent and to my friendly lumberjack, Rob. I also dedicate it to all the artists who have not gone to school and have enormous talent, and to anyone who has overcome addictions in their life.

My incredible gratitude goes to Judy Johnson for her amazing ability and insight to take my artwork and scripture and highlight them with color and imagination. Not only is she the design artist, she is now the publisher, also.

Last, but certainly not least, I would like to honor the memory of the late David Biebel. Without question, he was my hero. I believe God brought us together for a reason, and we discovered a connection in our family that we hadn't even known about before. David made many people's dreams become reality, including mine. He began the publication of this series, and even though he is now with the Lord, it will continue on.

*Dianne Jivari*

# Compliance

But those who trust in the Lord will find new strength.
They will soar high on wings like eagles.
They will run and not grow weary.
They will walk and not faint.
Isaiah 40:31

For just as the heavens are higher than the earth,
so my ways are higher than your ways
and my thoughts higher than your thoughts.
Isaiah 55:9

But blessed are those who trust in the Lord
and have made the Lord their hope and confidence.
Jeremiah 17:7

# Desire

May he grant your heart's desires
and make all your plans succeed.
Psalm 20:4

Take delight in the Lord,
and he will give you your heart's desires.
Psalm 37:4

We can make our plans,
but the Lord determines our steps.
Proverbs 16:9

# Destiny

But I, the Lord, search all hearts and examine secret motives.
I give all people their due rewards,
according to what their actions deserve.
Jeremiah 17:10

And we know that God causes everything to work together
for the good of those who love God
and are called according to his purpose for them.
Romans 8:28

Commit your actions to the Lord,
and your plans will succeed.
Proverbs 16:3

# Determination

So let's not get tired of doing what is good.
At just the right time we will reap a harvest of blessing if we don't give up.
Galatians 6:9

And I am certain that God, who began the good work within you,
will continue his work until it is finally finished
on the day when Christ Jesus returns.
Philippians 1:6

I have fought the good fight, I have finished the race,
and I have remained faithful.
2 Timothy 4:7

# Diligence

Lazy people want much but get little,
but those who work hard will prosper.
Proverbs 13:4

So let's not get tired of doing what is good.
At just the right time we will reap a harvest of blessing if we don't give up.
Galatians 6:9

Work hard and become a leader;
be lazy and become a slave.
Proverbs 12:24

# Dreams

Rejoice in our confident hope.
Be patient in trouble, and keep on praying.
Romans 12:12

Commit your actions to the Lord,
and your plans will succeed.
Proverbs 16:3

"For I know the plans I have for you," says the Lord.
"They are plans for good and not for disaster, to give you a future and a hope."
Jeremiah 29:11

# Envision

This vision is for a future time. It describes the end, and it will be fulfilled.
If it seems slow in coming, wait patiently, for it will surely take place.
It will not be delayed.
Habakkuk 2:3

And the Lord said to them, "Now listen to what I say:
If there were prophets among you,
I, the Lord, would reveal myself in visions.
I would speak to them in dreams."
Numbers 12:6

One night the Lord spoke to Paul in a vision and told him,
"Don't be afraid! Speak out! Don't be silent!"
Acts 18:9

# Fulfillment

It is pleasant to see dreams come true,
but fools refuse to turn from evil to attain them.
Proverbs 13:19

And the Lord said, "That's right, and it means that I am watching,
and I will certainly carry out all my plans."
Jeremiah 1:12

But it is the Lord who did just as he planned.
He has fulfilled the promises of disaster he made long ago.
Lamentations 2:17

# Goals

It is better to take refuge in the Lord
than to trust in people.
Psalm 118:8

But as for you, be strong and courageous,
for your work will be rewarded.
2 Chronicles 15:7

May he grant your heart's desires
and make all your plans succeed.
Psalm 20:4

# Impossibilities

"You don't have enough faith," Jesus told them. "I tell you the truth,
if you had faith even as small as a mustard seed, you could say to this mountain,
'Move from here to there,' and it would move. Nothing would be impossible."
Matthew 17:20


Jesus looked at them intently and said, "Humanly speaking, it is impossible.
But with God everything is possible."
Matthew 19:26


You can pray for anything, and if you have faith, you will receive it.
Matthew 21:22


For I can do everything through Christ, who gives me strength.
Philippians 4:13

# Longing

*I have tried hard to find you—
don't let me wander from your commands.*
Psalm 119:10

*Our hearts have not deserted you.
We have not strayed from your path.*
Psalm 44:18

*But as for you, be strong and courageous,
for your work will be rewarded.*
2 Chronicles 15:7

# Passion

He was the one who prayed to the God of Israel,
"Oh, that you would bless me and expand my territory!
Please be with me in all that I do,
and keep me from all trouble and pain!"
And God granted him his request.
1 Chronicles 4:10

But as for you, be strong and courageous,
for your work will be rewarded.
2 Chronicles 15:7

Commit your actions to the Lord,
and your plans will succeed.
Proverbs 16:3

# Prayer

The eyes of the Lord watch over those who do right;
his ears are open to their cries for help.
Psalm 34:15

O my God, lean down and listen to me. Open your eyes and see our despair.
See how your city—the city that bears your name—lies in ruins.
We make this plea, not because we deserve help, but because of your mercy.
Daniel 9:18

Listen to my voice in the morning, Lord.
Each morning I bring my requests to you and wait expectantly.
Psalm 5:3

# Pursuit

Whoever pursues righteousness and unfailing love
will find life, righteousness, and honor.
Proverbs 21:21

So then, let us aim for harmony in the church and try to build each other up.
Romans 14:19

But you, Timothy, are a man of God; so run from all these evil things.
Pursue righteousness and a godly life,
along with faith, love, perseverance, and gentleness.
1 Timothy 6:11

# Relentless

But we are not like those who turn away from God to their own destruction.
We are the faithful ones, whose souls will be saved.
Hebrews 10:39

Work hard so you can present yourself to God and receive his approval.
Be a good worker, one who does not need to be ashamed
and who correctly explains the word of truth.
2 Timothy 2:15

Always be joyful. Never stop praying. Be thankful in all circumstances,
for this is God's will for you who belong to Christ Jesus.
Do not stifle the Holy Spirit. Do not scoff at prophecies, but test everything that is said.
Hold on to what is good. Stay away from every kind of evil.
1 Thessalonians 5:16-22

# Shattered

*The sacrifice you desire is a broken spirit.
You will not reject a broken and repentant heart, O God.*
Psalm 51:17

*The Lord is close to the brokenhearted;
he rescues those whose spirits are crushed.*
Psalm 34:18

*He heals the brokenhearted
and bandages their wounds.*
Psalm 147:3

# Vision

Don't be like them, for your Father knows
exactly what you need even before you ask him!
Matthew 6:8

Even if we feel guilty, God is greater than our feelings,
and he knows everything.
1 John 3:20

The poor and the oppressor have this in common—
the Lord gives sight to the eyes of both.
Proverbs 29:13

Jesus told him, "I am the way, the truth, and the life.
No one can come to the Father except through me."
John 14:6

# Wishes

Keep on asking, and you will receive what you ask for. Keep on seeking, and you will find. Keep on knocking, and the door will be opened to you.
Matthew 7:7

He existed before anything else,
and he holds all creation together.
Colossians 1:17

But if you remain in me and my words remain in you,
you may ask for anything you want, and it will be granted!
John 15:7

# Healthy Life Press • Bristol, VA
## Books | eBooks

*A Small, Independent Christian Publisher with a big mission—to help people live healthier lives physically, emotionally, spiritually, and relationally.*

Visit *www.healthylifepress.com* to view all of our resources.

276-608-2086 | info@healthylifepress.com

www.ingramcontent.com/pod-product-compliance
Lightning Source LLC
Chambersburg PA
CBHW050748110526
44591CB00002B/15